Cybersecurity: A Business Solution

An executive perspective on managing cyber risk

by: **Rob Arnold**

Published By:

Threat Sketch, LLC
450 Design Ave.
Winston-Salem, NC 27016
ThreatSketch.com

Cover design by:

Lachelle Via
Charming Ink
http:/CharmingInk.com

ISBN-10: 069294415X

ISBN-13: 978-0692944158

Library of Congress Control Number: 2017913744

10 9 8 7 6 5 4 3 2 1

SHARING AND PURCHASING

Much time and money went into producing this book. I encourage sharing legitimately purchased, physical copies of this book, especially through libraries. I served on a local library board for a time and believe wholeheartedly in their mission. However, making and distributing digital copies is prohibited.

If you find yourself in possession of a digital copy and you are not sure if it was legitimately purchased, then please buy a copy of your own. I trust you to do the right thing, because good cybersecurity is rooted in a foundation of trust. Without trust we might as well not even bother.

Digital and print copies of this book are available from major booksellers and through our website:

http://CybersecurityABusinessSolution.com

Bulk purchasers, non-profits, and bonafide educational institutions are encouraged to request discounts or the rights to partial reprints. Likewise, commercial entities that would like to distribute print or digital copies (in whole or part) for the purpose of client education should request a licensing agreement. Please contact Threat Sketch through the website listed above to arrange suitable terms.

DEDICATION

In memory of my grandfathers.

Men who fought fiercely for their family and their country.

———

ACKNOWLEDGEMENTS

Many thanks to:

Susan, Kelly, Milla, Zach, Logan and our extended, blended family, all of whom gave me encouragement, sacrificed many mornings to my rants, and gave me space for my writing. My business partner Nathan, to whom I am forever indebted. My reviewers Angela, Bess, Dad, Chuck, Dan, Doug, Greg, Jaclyn, Joe, John, Roland, and Will, who helped shape the contents of this book. My editors Karen, Liz, and Myra, who kept me on task and on point. And cover designer, Lachelle, who wields creativity beyond measure.

Without your help this book would not exist.

CONTENTS

Introduction

———

Cyber attacks create a perfect storm of increased expenses and reduced revenue. Once an organization has been attacked, cash immediately flows out to pay for things like notifying customers, fending off lawsuits, and the resulting increased customer service costs. At the same time, revenues decrease as a result of lost productivity and lower sales that accompany damage to the organization's reputation.

The cybersecurity proposition is simple: Manage cyber risk to keep more profits and beat the odds that your organization will fold in the cash flow crisis caused by a cyber attack. But how do you know what risks your company is facing? How can you prepare for an attack? How much of your budget should be distributed among countless choices? Isn't all this just an IT problem that is best outsourced to technical experts? *Hint: It is not.*

This book is a guide for the leaders of small and medium businesses all of which are at risk of going bankrupt in the aftermath of a cyber attack. The goal is to help senior leadership understand the landscape of cybersecurity, which is a Wild West frontier that formed in the wake of ever-rising technology adoption. Cybersecurity risk must be addressed with more than just Information Technology (IT) solutions like firewalls and antivirus software. Organizations that embrace the new reality of our

Introduction

modern, technological world will also find a competitive edge in addressing cybersecurity — an edge that will set a company apart from its competitors and capture more market share. Those that do not sit like the proverbial frog in water that is slowly rising to a boil, never taking action until it is too late.

Chapter One

———

Background

This book is written specifically for you, an executive in a small or medium business that has decided to explore the topic of cybersecurity from a business perspective. By the term *executive* we mean someone with senior managerial responsibility in a business organization. In small companies, the executive role is not as clear as it is in large companies where titles like Chairman, CEO, and CFO plainly identify them. In small companies, the executives wear many hats. The founder of a small business, or partners in a small medical or legal firm, may consider themselves part of the front-line as well. Most days that is probably true, but someone must step out of the trenches and lead the company strategically. Occasionally, the sole-proprietor or solo-entrepreneur stops what he or she is doing to think about where the business is going and how to invest the next dollar. At that moment the entrepreneur becomes the *executive*, to whom this book is written, because he or she is the senior manager in charge of the company.

You may not realize it, but your role in managing cybersecurity is much more important than you think. Outsourcing the details of cybersecurity to technical experts is, one thing, but not doing your part and blindly handing off the problem to outsiders would be irresponsible.

Why Cybersecurity Matters for You

Your involvement matters because cybersecurity represents both an economic threat and a business trend that has emerged on *your* watch. In the last decade, the economics of cybersecurity changed the business landscape dramatically and you have a duty to manage this change. You also have a duty to recognize and manage anything that threatens the organization's welfare and its ecosystem.

Cybersecurity is tied closely to the advancement of technology. It lags only long enough for incentives like black markets to evolve and new exploits to be discovered. There is no end in sight for the advancement of technology, so we can expect the same from cybersecurity. It is a new facet of business that is here to stay and one that will evolve rapidly. Some executives will recognize this, embrace it early, and beat the competition. Others will be dragged kicking and screaming, or left for dead.

Decades ago cyber attacks were mostly pesky things that caused a few hours of downtime. It was common to hear small business executives say, "Our company is so small and my data so unimportant that no one would care." You cannot afford to think that way in today's world. An outdated view of cybersecurity and the false belief that no one cares about your company and the data you have is exactly what puts your organization at risk.

The economic impact of cyber attacks and the incentives for hackers are very different today, which is one reason even small businesses are vulnerable. This is because the information businesses collect, process, and exchange has become more valuable and easier to exploit for nefarious gain. Another factor is the liability created when this data comes into an organization's possession. Third is the trend toward hackers using automation to attack vulnerable small and medium businesses on an industrial scale. The convergence of these three trends means that modern attacks are more damaging than cyber attacks used to be, and it is almost certain they will occur on your watch.

Cyber Attacks in the Real World

Consider an employee's W-2 form. Before the 2000s, the information on this form had a nominal value that approached the price of the paper on which it was printed. There was no easy way to monetize a stolen W-2 form. Today, there is a thriving black market for personally identifiable information. As of 2017, the going price for a W-2 is between $4 and $20, depending on the income of the wage earner[1]. That may not seem like much, but it represents a massive increase from the two-cent value of a printed W-2 decades ago. Stealing even a single W-2 makes sense when attackers operate from a country where $20 is a full day's wages. Stealing them by the hundreds or thousands using automated attacks against scores of unsuspecting and unprepared small businesses makes even more sense for criminals anywhere in the world.

---

[1] Krebs, Brian. "Shopping for W2s, Tax Data on the Dark Web." *Krebs on Security*. 2017. https://krebsonsecurity.com/2017/01/shopping-for-w2s-tax-data-on-the-dark-web/.

Background

Having established why hackers are coming for your data, let's look at the damage done when they strike. Continuing with the W-2 theft example, state and federal laws require employers to report cyber theft, also known as a *data breach*. Failing to disclose the breach opens the door to class-action lawsuits where juries can award unlimited damages to victims due to your negligence. Disclosing the breach helps shield you and the organization from claims of negligence and in some cases will prevent class action suits. However, the organization will not be off the hook completely. Defending a non-class action lawsuit will costs tens of thousands of dollars, even if you win.

Additional costs include losses the employee will suffer if their identity is used to open credit in their name, drain their bank accounts, etc. Worse, the threat of identity theft will follow them forever. Related, indirect costs to the employer include replacing the employee if he or she quits and a reduction in morale among peer employees. It may become harder and more expensive to hire good talent, and customers hearing of the breach may look at competitors they believe are more vigilant.

A single stolen W-2 might net an attacker $20, but your organization and employees may be on the hook for tens or hundreds of thousands of dollars in damages. And this is just one example of how cyber attacks wreak havoc on an organization. Black markets and cyber espionage make seemingly mundane data worth stealing and exploiting. Trade secrets, access to bank accounts, and private communication are very lucrative targets. Sometimes it is not your own data, but a client's data accessible through you or your employees that is the target.

Cybersecurity: A Business Solution

Our highly connected, digital world has ushered in a new era of cyber crime. One that is growing fast and changing constantly. Executives who stick their head in the sand, try to keep a data breach a secret, pass off cybersecurity as just an IT problem, or wait for government protection will pay a steep price.

Many executives in the 1990s were adamant that computers were a novel expense that would never add real value to their business models. The idea that they would elevate the discussion of computers to an executive level was as absurd as typing their own email. Executives that clung to this view doomed their company to lose ground when competitors with forward-thinking executives raised technology to a boardroom discussion. Today cybersecurity is what computers were then. It is history, repeating itself and we already know who wins. Organizations led by executives that are willing to buck old-school thinking and grapple with the Wild West of cybersecurity will come out on top.

Today, the *outdated* view is thinking that cybersecurity is a technical problem best delegated to information technology (IT) experts. It goes hand-in-hand with the idea that cybersecurity involves only preventing attacks by anticipating them and implementing as many deterrents as possible. In contrast, a modern view of cybersecurity recognizes that countering every possible attack to achieve perfect security is financially unfeasible[2]. This new mindset also considers what happens *when* attacks occur, because

---

[2] Gordon, L. , Loeb, M. , Lucyshyn, W. and Zhou, L., "Externalities and the Magnitude of Cyber Security Underinvestment by Private Sector Firms: A Modification of the Gordon-Loeb Model." *Journal of Information Security*, 6, 24-30. doi: 10.4236/jis.2015.61003. 2015.

they will. Astute executives realize that spending every dime on prevention is futile and take a more holistic view of the problem.

Finding the right balance among various preventive and preparatory measures is like building an investment portfolio of stocks, bonds, and real estate. The right mix depends on what the external markets are doing and your appetite for taking risk. As time goes on the markets will change and your life circumstances change. Allocations in your portfolio adjust accordingly. This book is a guide to making investments in cybersecurity that reflect the external threat landscape, internal business strategy, and the organization's appetite for risk.

Despite having excellent cybersecurity teams and multi-million dollar budgets, large companies have learned that cybersecurity is a business problem that must be managed from the top. They have realized that outsourcing and delegation only goes so far when building a comprehensive cybersecurity plan and keeping it up to date as internal and external circumstances change. For the foreseeable future, the management of cybersecurity as a business problem will rest upon the shoulders of top management. Unless you embrace this new role, your organization will be a cybersecurity have-not in a time where data privacy and security is of increasing concern among clients and suppliers.

What happens if you do not step up to the plate? Well, according to a 2017 report[3], nearly one-quarter of small businesses

---

[3] "Second Annual State of Ransomware Report: US Survey Results," Osterman Research Inc. July 2017, https://www.malwarebytes.com/pdf/white-papers/SecondAnnualStateofRansomwareReport-USA.pdf

that suffered a ransomware attack were forced to immediately stop their operations. How long can your organization survive if revenue generating operations stopped abruptly while payroll and other expenses continued? What long-term damage will be done to your clients' perception of your organization's ability to offer uninterrupted service?

Savvy competitors simply wait for your market share to open up as a result of your inattention. On the flip side, effective management of cybersecurity is necessary just to stay on par with forward thinking competitors. Having a comprehensive cybersecurity plan in place can position your company to survive the same attacks that will bankrupt (or severely disrupt) your peers. When that happens *you* can pick up *their* market share and grow your company.

Another reason to take cybersecurity seriously at the executive level is that larger, cyber-savvy companies are often direct, or indirect, clients who take the security of their supply chain very seriously. Studies show that as many as 63 percent of data breaches are linked to a third-party[4], because weak downstream suppliers make great back doors into otherwise secure systems. In response to this, the NIST Cybersecurity Framework (a technical implementation guide) was recently revised to add emphasis to supply chain scrutiny, and an executive order from the

---

[4] "2013 Trustwave Global Security Report," Trustwave Document Library. https://www.trustwave.com/Resources/Library/Documents/2013-Trustwave-Global-Security-Report/

Background

White House[5] drove this same point home for government agencies. The government, their downstream contractors, and large private sector companies will begin culling lax suppliers and awarding business to those who demonstrate they take cybersecurity seriously. Nimble executives who address cybersecurity at their core will have an advantage — one that differentiates a company from its competitors and may command a premium. If you insist that your plate is full just managing what you already have, you will miss the opportunity to rise above your competitors, just like the old-school executives who refused to see technology as anything more than an expense.

Consumers have also become quite sensitive to cybersecurity, and it is reflected in their buying habits. Forward-thinking executives can capitalize on this trend too. A prominent example was Apple's stance on personal privacy when the FBI demanded they decrypt an iPhone used in a terrorist event[6]. Playing up their investments in encryption and demonstrating loyalty to a client even in the worst of times helped solidify consumer trust in Apple products. We would never advocate brinksmanship with the FBI, but Apple's response was a brilliant way to gain confidence among consumers. Learning to manage cybersecurity from a

---

[5] "Presidential Executive Order on Strengthening the Cybersecurity of Federal Networks and Critical Infrastructure," White House, Office of the Press Secretary, May 11, 2017, https://www.whitehouse.gov/the-press-office/2017/05/11/presidential-executive-order-strengthening-cybersecurity-federal

[6] "A Message to Our Customers," Apple, Inc., February 16, 2016, https://www.apple.com/customer-letter/

business perspective means you can spot and leverage opportunities like this too.

The Business of Cybersecurity

Funding higher levels of cybersecurity is part of the business problem executives must address. Small and medium businesses often operate on razor thin margins. Therefore, it is important to ensure every cybersecurity dollar is spent wisely. Failure to do so not only leaves gaps in security, but overspending can destroy a competitive edge on cost. When allocating funds it is important to decide which cybersecurity expenses are treated as a cost of goods sold and which to consider as investments for improving profits and winning market share. It is the same problem executives faced during the rise of computers and the Internet decades ago: "Is this newfangled stuff to be treated as an expense or an investment?" We argue that it is both and will help you understand both perspectives.

It is particularly hard for busy leaders of small companies to prioritize risk management planning. They want to jump to the part where they buy cybersecurity solutions and get back to running their business as quickly as possible. Taking time to think about strategy, for a small company, seems like a waste of time when there are customers waiting to be served. But nothing could be further from the truth, and we also understand that it can be daunting to think about cybersecurity when everything is so technical. Separating the business parts from implementation details helps address technical anxieties and it is an important theme throughout the book. We use the terms *strategy* and *tactical* to identify those areas that need your attention and which to consider delegating or outsourcing.

Strategy refers to high-level planning and management. Setting goals and managing toward them with clear budgets and priorities is a strategic duty, but there are others. Determining an acceptable level of risk, encouraging employees to take cybersecurity seriously, managing contractual liability, and protecting the reputation of the company are a few examples. Other roles and duties will emerge in later chapters as we cover different aspects of managing cyber risk.

Tactical refers to using a special skill, or competence, to dive deeply into a specific area of concern. Tactical solutions are the building blocks with which a strategic plan is implemented each playing a specific function within a larger strategy. Tactical cybersecurity functions include IT, legal, accounting, insurance, and other specialties that can be applied to reduce risk. Each plays a role in preventing attacks and reducing the impact of adverse events.

Before we dive into our step-by-step explanation of your role, let's examine several of the contributions and benefits to executive involvement. Most of these functions are impossible to outsource because they require expertise and authority that only top management possesses. That doesn't mean you cannot use tools and advisors to help you along the way, it just means you cannot relinquish responsibility for them.

Stating and controlling direction. Goal setting starts at the top and reflects the needs of the business. Goals and objectives provide context for tactical planning and communicating them clearly to a diverse team of expert tactical advisors keeps everyone focused, and on the same page.

Cybersecurity: A Business Solution

Allocating budget. Business owners understand that cybersecurity measures will cost time and money, and as an executive, it is your responsibility to decide where the money will go. Your IT guru recommends a new firewall. Then your insurance agent recommends adding a cyber insurance policy. If you buy both (and you should buy both), how do you divide up the limited budget between all the possible solutions? If cybersecurity is relegated to just a tactical IT problem, you will have a fantastic firewall but no protection when a hacker finds their way around it.

Authorizing company-wide policies. Whether it's enforcing bring-your-own-device policies or using strong passwords, someone should be in control of what's being done and how well policies are being followed. The ability to authorize new cybersecurity measures comes from the top in any organization. The people-driven aspects of cybersecurity are absolutely a business problem that you, as the top manager, need to oversee.

Maintaining compliance. Once authorized, policies and procedures must be carried out. Failure to do so will be construed as negligence, which leads to prosecution and regulatory fines. Cyber insurance, citing "failure to follow" exclusions, will also deny coverage if you fail to maintain your own security standards[7]. Your authority and your ability to develop a culture of compliance is critical to avoiding these catastrophic mistakes.

Empathy in a crisis. When a data breach happens, despite every effort to prevent it, clients and employees will be more

---

[7] "Avoiding the Most Common Cyber Insurance Claim Denials," GB&A, https://www.gbainsurance.com/avoiding-cyber-claim-denials

forgiving if they believe top management was paying attention and making effort. Even when responsibility for a breach can be traced to an individual or external actor, clients and employees want to know that *you* were being vigilant.

Justify spending. The return on investment for cybersecurity is obscured. It is hard to measure how bad things could have been if you did not invest in something that prevents or reduces loss, but that does not mean it is impossible. Risk management tools and techniques that have been adapted to cybersecurity can rationalize spending. Whether you report to yourself or another stakeholder in the company, you can invest with confidence when you can articulate the value.

The chapters that follow provide a non-technical, effective way to approach your role in managing cybersecurity and explain the tools available to help you. We will not go deeply into tactical details that can be delegated to staff and vendors, although we will explain what they are and how they get used so you can manage them effectively. If you happen to be a technology whiz, and want to dig into the details, there is a white paper that goes along with this book that introduces the NIST Cybersecurity Framework[8]. That framework will let you explore the technical side as deeply as you would like. However, the aim of this book is to provide a clear understanding of how to define, view and manage cyber risk from a business perspective. The technical aspects are only discussed to help you manage those contributions as part of a larger whole.

---

[8] Download companion material from http://CybersecurityABusinessSolution.com

Chapter Two

———

Strategic Cyber Risk Management

Strategic management of cybersecurity is where you, as a small or medium business executive, should focus your attention. Even if you do not have any technical skills, you still play an important role and have much to contribute. This chapter explains the correct way to approach cybersecurity and provides a tutorial on objectively measuring risk. In this chapter, you will learn the correct way for business executives to approach cybersecurity. In addition to explaining the process, you'll find an overview of objectively measuring risk, which will help as you move forward in your planning and decision making.

A Word About Compliance

Compliance is an important tool, but it is rarely a solution by itself. The problem lies in the common misconception that audit- or checklist-based compliance demonstrates both sufficient involvement and fiduciary responsibility. Leaders who fall prey to this genuinely (but falsely) believe the organization is very secure. However, when events play out as described below, compliance will not save the company. While audits and checklist are important, they are not enough to completely fill the duty you inherited.

For some businesses, parts of cybersecurity are dictated by regulations mandated by specific organizations or governing bodies. The important thing to remember about all regulations is that they are developed or required by a third party that has different strategic objectives than your organization. When dealing with regulations, executives must pay close attention to the difference between the goals of the regulatory authority and the goals of the company. Even when they are an "industry standard" there is a need to keep a close eye on where regulatory compliance does not fulfill a company's individual cybersecurity needs.

Compliance Versus Exposure

A common example of a cybersecurity regulation is the Payment Card Industry Data Security Standard (PCI DSS), which are regulations that apply to any organization that accepts credit cards. The regulations emerged to protect credit card processors and merchant banks. The focus is on *their* exposure through your operations. Also, while the regulations are effective for securing credit card transactions and related data, trying to apply them across an entire organization would make operations too cumbersome and expensive. The cost of security must be weighed against the cost of revenue generating activity. That includes lost productivity for cumbersome procedures.

Another example is the Health Insurance Portability and Accountability (HIPAA), which applies to the medical industry. A doctor's office may have achieved compliance and created forms that explain HIPAA to patients and collect the appropriate signatures, which are kept on file to prove compliance. In the meantime, they are collecting patients' social security numbers, dates of birth, and insurance policy numbers. This information might get stored in a server with sub-par security – meaning sub-par in relation to actual risk, yet on-par with HIPAA requirements. While the office feels like it is secure because they followed HIPAA rules, they are still open to hackers stealing and selling patients' personal information. When a data breach happens, a court may not find them negligent due to their compliance, but the reputational damage among patients may be enough to bankrupt the practice.

The takeaway is that while checklist-based regulations provide a good start for security and cover their own objectives well, they present a trap for executives, leading to a feeling that the business is protected from cyber attack, when in fact it might be only a small part of what is needed. Audit and checklist driven regulatory compliance is not enough to achieve cybersecurity. It may be enough to sufficiently secure one area of operation, but no checklist can keep up with the constantly changing landscape of cybersecurity that an organization faces. You are ultimately responsible for what happens. Being compliant may reduce liability, but it will not keep attacks from happening or shield the organization from potentially devastating harm.

While the axiom holds that you will ultimately be responsible for what happens to the company, there is an emerging standard that is both a regulatory target and a good way to approach cybersecurity. It is the NIST Cybersecurity Framework, which strives to be both a risk management program and a technical guide to implementing strong cybersecurity controls. The NIST

Cybersecurity Framework does contain an extensive checklist which is referred to as a "Profile" in the documentation. But it also demands that high-level strategic risk management be part of the implementation.

The NIST Framework will quickly overwhelm anyone without a technical background. However, alongside the technical advice in the NIST Framework are directives that top leadership must play an active role in managing cyber risk. What exactly that means to resource constrained small or medium businesses executives is precisely what we aim to illustrate.

Cyber Risk Management

Risk management is a holistic approach to reducing both the likelihood of adverse events and their impact. This strategy recognizes that winning *every* skirmish (when the hackers need only win once) is financially infeasible, if not impossible. Methods to reduce the cost and duration of a successful attack are considered alongside, or as alternatives to, expensive defenses. A risk management approach also means looking for more than just technical solutions. Holistic plans will reduce risk by using legal, financial, insurance, and other non-IT methods to manage the problem effectively. Applying tried and true techniques of risk management, which are well established in other fields, is the correct way to approach cybersecurity.

Table 2.1 lists the goals for strategically managing cyber risk. Communicating these goals is a critical function, and executive authority is required to cement them in place.

Table 2.1 – Strategic Goals

Goals

G1 Reduce the potential for losses from cyber attacks to an acceptable level.

G2 Align cybersecurity efforts with the business mission.

G3 Identify and meet mandatory regulatory requirements.

G4 Exploit opportunities to position cyber risk investments for gains in profit or market share.

G5 Adapt cybersecurity over time to reflect changes in business strategy, changes in the risk landscape, and lessons learned.

The strategies for meeting the goals in Table 2.1 include the items below. Some will be themes, chapters, or sections within this book. Others appear as milestones in the larger risk management plan that we advocate.

- Examine the cybersecurity landscape and determine risk appetite.
- Engage a diverse team of expert advisors from many fields.
- Balance spending between prevention and preparedness.
- Allocate more resources to threats posing the highest overall risk.
- Address the most likely and most damaging threats first.

Keep in mind that what we present here is suitable for profit-based companies. Some parts of the strategy may overlap with what works for nonprofits and governments, but things start to diverge when descending into the specifics. In some ways, cyber risk management is easier among for-profits simply because motivation can be boiled down to dollars and cents.

That being said, even among traditional profit-based companies cybersecurity is not a one-size-fits-all endeavor. Those companies that closely identify with social causes or utility production of a critical service will need to pay more attention to the external value of their goods, services, and supply chains. Later chapters will cover external value in more depth, but how one looks at the value of data begins to illustrate why cybersecurity strategies differ vastly from one organization to the next.

The goals and strategies outlined above are designed to help you establish an economically sound skeleton, or blueprint, that is unique to your business strategy. The tactical team of experts will fill this in with specific solutions and advice. A properly designed skeleton will provide support for business needs while withstanding forces applied by external threats.

The tools and tactics in Table 2.2 are what you will use to build the strategic framework and oversee implementation of a cybersecurity plan that fits your organization's unique disposition. In some cases, like an audit, you will delegate the execution. But knowing when to do an audit and what to do with the results still requires executive involvement. Treating delegation of these duties as a blind hand-off is a recipe for failure.

Table 2.2 – Tools and Tactics

Tools and Tactics	
• Strategic Cyber Risk Assessments • Budget Size • Budget Allocations • Priorities • Audits and Vulnerability Assessments	• Communication • Contracts • Policies • Training • Culture

With one or two exceptions, you will undoubtedly recognize every item in Table 2.2 as a managerial topic you have encountered before. Though you understand audits well enough, vulnerability assessments may be unfamiliar. In short, a vulnerability assessment is a specific type of audit that enumerates all the holes and flaws in a given system. In theory, if you closed every hole you would be safe from attack. But assessments are incapable of testing for unknown flaws and new exploits are being developed daily, so they can never be 100 percent complete.

As assessment accuracy increases, the cost to identify and fix every flaw becomes quite steep, and the solutions often drag on productivity. There is a break-even point for chasing prevention, and what hangs below that point is a *residual risk* that must still be managed.

Later chapters will dig deeper into the use of audits and vulnerability assessments, but first, we will explain strategic cyber risk assessments. The strategic cyber risk assessment is an important executive decision-making tool that harnesses the mathematical properties of risk. To help you understand these important properties we will give you a short lesson on measuring risk. Don't worry though, the real-world strategic cyber risk assessments will not require that you do the calculations on your own.

The Basics of Measuring Risk

There are four fundamental forces involved in risk management, which also apply to cybersecurity. They are assets, impact, threats, and likelihood. You have internal knowledge of and a fair amount of control over *assets*, which are tangible and intangible things that have value. You also have some control over *impact*, which refers to loss of, or damage to, an asset. However, *threats* that represent adversaries and their methods of attack are external to your control. *Likelihood* is the wild card in the bunch. Likelihoods determine if and when a threat will materialize, succeed, and do damage. While never fully under your control, likelihoods can be shaped and influenced to manage the risk.

Mathematically, the forces can be represented in a formula such as:

$$\text{Risk} = p(\text{Asset, Threat}) \times d(\text{Asset, Threat})$$

where p() is the likelihood that a Threat will materialize/succeed against an Asset, and d() is the likelihood of various levels of damage that may occur. Of course, we are also interested in managing the Risk side of the equation. The value of Risk is influenced by all of the terms and functions on the right side. For instance, reducing the impact of damages is as effective as altering the likelihood that an attack will materialize when the goal is to reduce overall risk.

Evaluating these trade-offs helps executives make better investment decisions.

The mathematical properties are useful because they represent a powerful way to make objective decisions about priorities and the allocation of resources to reduce overall risk. To illustrate, consider a simple two-threat scenario[9].

- There is a 20% chance that Threat X will do $1M damage
- There is a 10% chance that Threat Y will do $10M damage

Armed with this information, you might place greater priority on Threat X due to its higher likelihood of occurrence. However, Threat Y might be allocated more of the overall budget because the damage potential is higher. A more sophisticated view is to compare the two based on overall risk, which is $200K (20% x $1M) for Threat X, and $1M (10% x $10M) for Threat Y. This allows a direct comparison between them.

The actual math and statistics used are more complex, but the fundamentals are the same. Unless you happen to have a knack for statistics and the time to collect and interpret the data necessary to develop your own risk models you are better off using an off-the-shelf strategic cyber risk assessment that does the math and provides the data for you.

---

[9] To keep the math simple and easy to follow, we use a single percentage to represent chance rather than more complex probability curves.

The reason strategic cyber risk assessments (or just risk assessments) are so important is how their output shapes your understanding of the risk landscape and how it helps establish budgets and priorities among all the risks that are competing against you. Risk assessments are the lens through which executives can manage cybersecurity most effectively.

The website for this book links to an example report from a basic Threat Sketch Cyber Risk Assessment[10]. The basic assessment takes about twenty minutes to complete and is designed to capture knowledge about the organization's intangible asset profile and map this to relevant cybercrime statistics. It is an easy way to get a handle on the current landscape and is an excellent way to communicate to your tactical advisors where you need them to focus their initial effort. As such, a strategic cyber risk assessment forms a sort of Rosetta Stone for translating between business strategy and technical cyber-threats. The threat categories are the technical side of the translation, while budget allocations and priorities that reflect asset allocations are the strategic management side. The example report also includes a peer analysis, which is helpful when identifying opportunities for gain within the risk landscape.

Strategic and Tactical Planning

Cybersecurity presents a bit of a chicken-or-egg dilemma because just as strategic planning plays an important role in directing the tactical plans, the reverse is also true. Strategic

---

[10] Download companion material from http://CybersecurityABusinessSolution.com

answers to certain questions sometimes rely on the answers to tactical questions. Figure 2.A illustrates how tools and tactics at each level depend on input from the other. The correct way to unravel the co-dependency is to start with key strategic steps, have tactical experts do research, then return to the strategic level to complete the cycle. The process of kick-starting a cybersecurity initiative this way is what we refer to as *exploring risk*.

Figure 2.A - Strategic and tactical tools work together in a loop.

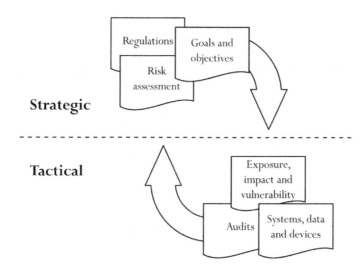

Exploring risk involves doing research and postponing the purchase and implementation of security controls. This research-only step reveals the complete picture of an organization's cyber risk. It will also achieve goals G2 and G3 from Table 2.1 and put a dollar figure on "acceptable level of risk" (also called *risk appetite*), which is part of G1.

Figure 2.B – Exploratory research of risk determines specific objectives that follow.

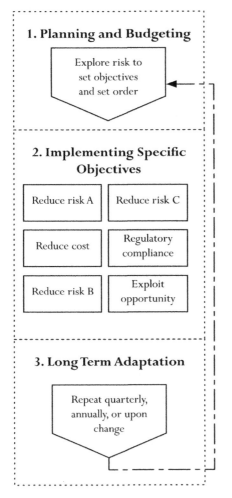

After exploring the tactical risks, you will return to the strategic tools and tactics with the information necessary to complete the remaining goals. Specifically, you will have a categorical list of threats to be addressed and regulations to be met, which become your next objectives. The strategic tools prioritize them and allocate funds appropriately among them. From there, your role is then to fund and oversee implementation by the appropriate tactical experts. Once these implementations have reduced risk to an acceptable level, you are free to pursue other objectives like finding opportunities for gain.

Figure 2.B depicts this process, which is divided into three main stages. The first stage involves taking strategic and tactical steps toward developing the plans and budget allocations that give definition to the second stage. Execution of the second stage is predominantly a technical endeavor, but guided by executive strategies and monitored with strategic tools. The third stage is the repetition of this process over time to detect and respond to any changes in the (tactical) external risk landscape and/or (strategic) internal organizational changes. The first time through this process may be daunting, but after the initial plans are in place it becomes very easy to repeat.

You will notice in Figure 2.B that in the middle stage nothing is prioritized, every objective is depicted equally, and the risks are shown as abstract letters. That is intentional because the first stage explores the risk landscape to develop plans and allocate rough budgets for the second stage. The vast majority of this book, and the bulk of your executive effort will be dedicated to executing the first stage. Responsibility for implementing specific, tactical objectives will primarily fall to staff and vendors. But there are a few tactical components for which you, as an executive, will be responsible. Chapter Seven will discuss these areas of responsibility.

Objectives and Milestones

The steps to explore risk and the steps to achieve specific risk management objectives all follow roughly the same path. We present this path as a series of milestones in Table 2.3 below. Throughout the book, we discuss how repetition of this mini-plan, with differing objectives, forms the backbone of cyber risk management.

Table 2.3 – Risk Management Milestones With Clear Role Assignments

	Milestone	Primary Role
M1	Set a Risk Management Objective	Strategic
M2	Conduct a Strategic Cyber Risk Assessment	Strategic
M3	Engage the Tactical Advisory Team	Tactical/Dual
M4	Tactical Assessments - Technical, Legal, Financial, and Insurance	Tactical
M5	Plan and Budget	Tactical/Dual
M6	Implement and Repeat	Tactical/Dual

Depending on the objective and context a milestone may be skipped or the work done in a previous iteration can be substituted. This is why we said all objectives follow "roughly" the same path. We present the whole plan with all milestones in their correct order below and a brief description of each follows. The remaining chapters will walk you through all of the steps in detail.

M1 - Set a Risk Management Objective: This is always set by the strategic advisory team, and common mistakes include setting overly broad objectives, assuming everyone is on the same page and failing to create a measurable definition for success. The key to success is setting narrow objectives with clear measurements of success.

M2 - Conduct a Strategic Cyber Risk Assessment: Use this to guide effort and allocation of resources. It provides context for the objective set in item one.

M3 - Engage the Tactical Advisory Team: This team goes well beyond traditional IT roles encompassing diverse advisors from many fields. Even the solo entrepreneur will need experts in diverse fields to accomplish this milestone. The exact makeup will vary based on the objective. A medium sized company's team might include mostly staff, while a small business may rely on vendors, mentors, and professional advisors to fill out the team.

M4 - Tactical Assessments - Technical, Legal, Financial, and Insurance: Use tactical tools and techniques to catalog and assess the current situation. It involves not only figuring out how to stop attacks, but also how to recover from attacks that happen despite best efforts. When exploring risk, the organization's total exposure will emerge here, and will likely be much larger than anyone expected.

M5 - Plan and Budget: The strategic priorities and budget allocations from M2 provide context for this planning. The results of milestone four will help size the budget and keep resource utilization and spending in line with expectations.

M6 - Implement and Repeat: Most parts will be technical, but some parts require executive attention. The measure of success defined in M1 marks the successful completion of this final milestone. Repetition will be in response to either internal or external changes and Chapter Seven will discuss how to detect changes in the risk landscape.

The time it takes to complete each milestone will vary according to the size of your business. A solo-entrepreneur might work through the process in a few hours divided up over coffee breaks, emails, and phone calls. For a mid-sized company, formal meetings might be warranted for each milestone. The formality of execution is not important. What is critical for success is that the milestones are done in the correct order, by people wearing the right hats, using tools and tactics appropriate to the task at hand. Equally critical is setting the right objective, which is milestone number one and the subject of the next chapter.

Chapter Three

———

Objectives and Risk Assessments

M1: Setting Objectives

Setting an objective and leading your advisory team toward that objective is a critical strategic contribution[11]. It does not require technical IT or cybersecurity knowledge, but it does require the skills and authority of a strategic leader. Skipping this step, or assuming everyone already knows the objective, is a common executive mistake when managing risk, and cybersecurity is no exception.

The basic choices for clear strategic objectives for cyber risk management are:

- Exploring risk - Identifying threats and measuring exposure
- Regulatory compliance - Meeting industry or government mandates

---

[11] Feliciano, Dan, "Why are Goals and Objectives Important?" Fast Company, April 2008, https://www.fastcompany.com/795028/why-are-goals-and-objectives-important.

- Reducing risk - Lessening exposure, limiting losses, and recovering from attacks
- Controlling costs - Achieving the best cost/benefit ratio from risk management expenses
- Identifying opportunities - Seeking gains, or a competitive edge, within the risk landscape

To ensure success for your organization, focus on one objective at a time instead of making an elaborate plan with multiple objectives. It is much better to string many small, focused objectives together even when tackling multiple goals. Taking on too much in a single step is a recipe for disaster. Later chapters will cover this in more detail.

Exploring risk is the starting point introduced in the previous chapter. The aim of this objective is to examine the entirety of the risk landscape. This is the first objective you work through, and then you will repeat this objective on a quarterly or annual basis. The first time aligns business strategy with cybersecurity efforts. Subsequent repetitions alert you to emerging risks or major shifts among the risks, which signal the need to update plans.

Regulatory compliance is a narrow objective for dealing with regulations that apply to an organization. Once in place, regulatory compliance becomes an integral part of the cybersecurity plan. Special regulatory considerations are discussed in subsequent chapters.

Reducing risk is broad in scope because it spans all potential threats. To achieve an appropriately small scope, you will focus on a single categorical threat as illustrated in the center of Figure 2.B, where each risk is addressed as a discrete step. The threat categories themselves are defined by the risk assessment which we discuss below.

Controlling costs is a straightforward concept, but it is not easy to balance with the other objectives. A cost control initiative makes sense if, for instance, there is a major drop in revenue or call for across-the-board cost cuts. If your company's strategy is to be the low-cost leader, routinely evaluating cyber risk with this objective might be a wise choice.

Identifying opportunities in the risk landscape is a way to gain profit or market share within the risk landscape. Apple's response to the FBI, highlighted in Chapter One, is one example of using cybersecurity to differentiate from the competition. Providing security for client data that exceeds expectations, or that meets a client's own regulatory requirements, can often command a premium. Likewise, promoting stronger security can attract market share.

If there is anything you might find fun about cybersecurity it is likely to be identifying opportunities for gain. Finding opportunities engages a much broader tactical team of advisors and encourages outside-the-box thinking. But you will want to make sure the organization is doing everything it can to manage downside risks first. Until the company has addressed all the categorical risks it faces, we do not recommend pursuing this objective. Executives that work diligently to arrive at this point are the true visionaries who will lead the pack.

A well-crafted objective will state what is to be accomplished through the cybersecurity plan *and* establish how to measure completion. For example, a cost control objective might specify a 10 percent reduction in current spending as the measure of success. A regulatory compliance objective might set passing an external audit as the benchmark for success. Clear, measurable objectives are easier to manage and better communicate expectations to everyone involved.

If you are addressing cybersecurity as a business problem for the first time, your starting objective will be exploring risk. We examine the remaining milestones from Table 2.3 from this perspective. Along the way, we also point out how to approach the milestones differently when the objective is something other than exploring risk.

Once you have selected exploring risk as the objective, you must provide a measure of success. In this case, the measure of success is:

> *Potential catastrophic losses will be determined and broken down into a manageable number (10-20) of high-level threat categories. Applicable regulatory requirements will also be identified. A plan to address each threat category and regulatory requirement will be developed. The plan will incorporate priorities and resource allocations that reflect the external cybersecurity landscape and strategic business objectives.*

Milestone two uses a strategic cyber risk assessment to identify top-level threats, priorities, and budget allocations that guide the exploration. The tactical advisory team, assembled as part of milestone three, will use this information to guide their effort. Priorities will let them know what to research first and budget allocations will tell them how much time to spend researching the impact of each categorical threat. However, there are other benefits to using this important tool when creating a holistic cybersecurity plan.

M2: Strategic Cyber Risk Assessments

Strategic cyber risk assessments offer several advantages to the executive. Any one of them is reason enough to consider learning how to use this tool. When you realize several advantages at once, the value increases exponentially. The benefits of a risk assessment for executives include:

- Engagement - Tangible proof that the executive team is addressing cybersecurity
- Strategic alignment - Cybersecurity efforts match strategic business goals
- Justification - Clear understanding of the value proposition for risk reduction efforts
- Priorities - Objectively determine which areas of risk are the most urgent to resolve
- Budget allocation - Distribute limited time and resources across all areas of risk

The output of a cyber risk assessment plays a role in meeting all five goals outlined in the previous chapter. It does this by serving four critical functions that facilitate executive strategies for managing cyber risk.

Communication. The results of a cyber risk assessment help communicate the needs of the organization to a diverse team of advisory experts from multiple disciplines. Priorities that rise from the assessment say what to do first, and suggested budgets indicate how much effort and expense should be allocated to each.

Context. As mentioned above, the priorities and budget guidance that comes out of a strategic cyber risk assessment give context to the objective. The tactical team uses priorities to align everyone's effort and the budget sets boundaries to keep spending in check.

Monitor progress. Results from a cyber risk assessment provide an early warning system for detecting when the risk management initiative is off track. Sometimes this indicates a problem, such as a vendor pushing priority and budget changes to meet a sales goal. In other cases, it uncovers a legitimate disconnect between the base assumptions made during a high-level analysis of risk and the reality of operations in the trenches. Either way, if there is a big discrepancy between the strategic priorities and allocations when compared to the tactical plans of an organization, further investigation is prudent.

Measured results. Priorities and budgets also serve as a yardstick for measuring success. Results from a cyber risk assessment give executives the ability to manage risk according to a concrete plan. Managing to this plan lets everyone know when they on the right track. Furthermore, executives that report to a higher authority can provide evidence that they are managing cyber risk appropriately.

It is also important to use the right risk assessment for your business. You will find a number of different cyber risk assessments on the market. Before deciding on one, make sure it's designed for your type and size of business. Small businesses cannot afford complex assessments that require a lot of input from internal and external analysts. Custom-built assessments may be more accurate, but the cost for that extra accuracy can be tens or hundreds of thousands of dollars. A related problem is sourcing and interpreting data for the analysis. Most small companies do not have data scientists and trained risk analysts on staff. If a cyber risk assessment does not come with threat categories and matching data to derive likelihood functions you will have to supply them.

Whatever strategic cyber risk assessment you choose, make sure the output supports you in achieving the goals and strategies outlined in Table 2.1. The previous chapter referenced a sample strategic cyber risk assessment available on the website for this book[12]. If you have not already done so, please review that now. While formats will differ from solution to solution, the key questions the assessment should answer are:

- What are the categorical threats?
- Which threat categories will have the most impact?
- Which threat categories will we encounter most frequently?

The answers to these questions will let you provide the tactical advisory team with more than just a list of objectives. You will be able to say which objectives are the most urgent and which should get the most attention. Because the answers to these questions are based on a profile of the business and its market

---

[12] Download companion material from http://CybersecurityABusinessSolution.com

strategy, they will automatically align tactical effort and expense with the business needs of the organization.

One example of a strategic cybersecurity risk assessment designed for small to medium businesses is the Threat Sketch Risk Assessment. It was specifically designed for busy executives without a technical background. A 20-minute survey captures a profile of the business strategy as it relates to intangible assets. Cybercrime statistics are then applied to the profile to produce a basic overview of the risk landscape. Advanced versions of the Threat Sketch Risk Assessment use more extensive surveys and incorporate more organizational details to produce additional information. However, the basic Threat Sketch Risk Assessment is a good way to get started and, as of this writing, it is free[13].

Other "free" alternatives include NIST's Special Publication 800-30, OCTAVE Allegro, and the Federal Financial Institutions Examination Council's (FFIEC) Cybersecurity Risk Assessment Tool. Each of these outline how to do a cyber risk assessment from scratch, but they require a level of expertise and time commitment that is substantial. Larger companies that have access to talented cybersecurity and business analysts, statistical expertise, and good sources of data will find these alternatives a good fit. A custom cyber risk assessment based on these alternatives may provide more granularity, but they all require significant internal resources. They are free to download, but not free to implement.

As you research options, be aware that many tools that are labeled as cyber risk assessments are not what we have described

---

[13] https://ThreatSketch.com

here. Very often vulnerability assessments, audits, checklists, and situational assessments are labeled as cyber risk assessments. The confusing labels are because terminology in the cybersecurity industry is not well standardized.

Even at this early point in the process the second stage of Figure 2.B, implementing specific objectives, is starting to take shape. Table 3.1 shows how the output of a risk assessment establishes the first draft of a strategic plan that will be handed off to the tactical advisory team in the next chapter.

Table 3.1 – Strategic risk assessment output as an early stage plan.

Objective	Priority	Budget
Reduce Risk – Website Attacks	1	66%
Reduce Risk – Point of Sale Hacks	2	34%

The above example is abbreviated to depict only two main threats. A full example, based on the Threat Sketch strategic cyber risk assessment, would include more threat categories. In later stages, we will also incorporate some of the other objectives discussed in the beginning of this chapter as well. However, just having the major threats identified goes a long way toward directing next efforts. The budget information that comes from the risk assessment will give the tactical advisors an idea as to how much effort they will put on researching vulnerabilities and impact when the process reaches chapter five.

The next milestone is to engage the tactical advisors. After going through a cybersecurity risk assessment, you have almost everything you need to direct a diverse team of experts toward the remaining milestones. You have a clear objective, you have a measure of success for the objective, and you have priorities and budget recommendations that reflect the internal business mission and the external threat landscape. The only thing lacking is a solid understanding of how and why the organization needs to balance preventive solutions with solutions that help prepare for the impact of an attack. The next chapter will cover this topic thoroughly so you can better direct the advisory team you are about to assemble.

Chapter Four

———

Prevention and Preparedness

Chasing complete security is not financially viable. Therefore, there must be a tradeoff between preventing attacks and preparing for the attacks that materialize despite best efforts. As part of the planning process, it is very important that you pay close attention to how your advisory team will address both aspects of risk. It also underscores the need for a much more diverse team. You can no longer place all of the responsibility solely on your IT guru. This chapter covers these topics in depth so that you have the information you need to guide the tactical advisory team's effort as they move forward.

Balancing Prevention and Preparedness

Prevention refers to everything done before an attacker successfully breaches an organization. Preparedness refers to things that should be in place to use after a breach is detected. Table 4.1 maps these terms to the functional areas of cyber risk management. These functional areas map directly to the NIST Cybersecurity Framework, but we approach them from a business angle in this chapter. For more about the relationship of this book to the NIST

Cybersecurity Framework, there is a white paper available as part of the companion material for this book[14].

Table 4.1 – A Quick Glance: Prevention vs. Preparedness

Prevention

    Identify potential risks and pending attacks

    Protect against or limit attacks

Preparedness

    Detect successful attacks

    Respond to an attack and limit loss

    Recover from the attack

If a company is to maximize the chance of survival in an uncertain world, then it is the executive's job to balance investments in both prevention and preparedness. Vendors and their solutions typically fall into one category or the other, though sometimes a solution can span both. Generally speaking, you will find IT folks are focused on prevention, but they are also involved in some technical aspects of preparedness as well.

One of the most common mistakes, especially among smaller companies, is to put all cybersecurity effort and money into prevention. This is symptomatic of the thinking that cybersecurity

---

[14] Download companion material from http://CybersecurityABusinessSolution.com

is an IT problem, rather than recognizing it as a business problem. Additionally, the money and effort needed to totally secure an organization from all possible attacks are infinitely high. Even if you spent every penny of your company's revenue on cybersecurity, you still could not guarantee 100 percent protection. That's why preparedness is just as important to the equation as prevention.

Regardless of how much you choose to spend on cybersecurity, it is important to make sure you don't put all your eggs in one basket, either prevention or preparedness. Typically an organization allocates between 20 to 50 percent of the budget to prevention, and usually on the lower end of that scale. The balance then goes toward preparedness.

The more certain one is that all threats are known and all possible attacks can be thwarted, the more one might allocate to prevention. With rare exceptions, allocating more than 50 percent of the overall budget to prevention would leave an organization open to losses in the event an attacker were to slip through even the best defenses.

The executive's role is to make sure that spending does not shift too much to one side or the other. An overzealous IT vendor might believe they can protect the company from all harm, leading to an over-investment in prevention. Likewise, an insurance agent might convince you that a large cybersecurity policy is all you need. Many executives honestly believe they are fully protected by either their IT staff/vendor, or an elaborate insurance policy. Neither case is correct. The truth lies somewhere in between.

Prevention

Anything that helps predict or prevent a pending attack is part of the prevention plan. In the next chapter, we outline how your advisory team will assess the vulnerability of key systems, services, etc. Vulnerabilities are flaws, backdoors, misconfigurations, etc., that determine which prevention measures are needed. Once the team knows where the flaws are, and knows which threats are the most pressing, it is much easier to decide which holes to plug.

Most companies can strike Predicting Threats off the list if they follow the advice in this book. However, there are still other options available if you have budget dollars to spare. There are advanced systems that use artificial intelligence and real-time threat intelligence to adaptively counter some attacks. These systems aren't foolproof, but if you can afford them they add an extra layer of predictive protection. Hopefully, these systems will continue to fall in price and be affordable to small businesses soon.

Below are some common examples of what your tactical team of advisors will suggest as preventive measures. It is by no means exhaustive. Because every organization is unique, the specific solutions will vary from company to company. The intent here is to help you understand the types of risk controls to expect in each category.

Cybersecurity: A Business Solution

Identify

- Strategic risk assessments - Identify assets at risk and major attack patterns
- Vulnerability scans - Finds holes in your website, network, software, etc.
- Asset management - Regular inventories and inspections that will reveal tampering, theft, etc.
- Audits – Checklists and guides to "best practices" can help identify areas of improvement.

Protect

- Data security - Examples include encryption, safe destruction, removable media management
- System maintenance - Keep software and hardware up to date (often referred to as "patching")
- Identity management and access controls - Usernames and passwords, and who has access to what data, files, and communications
- Firewall - Prevents hackers from having free reign of your network
- SPAM and virus filters - Block malicious attachments and software from running; reduce socially engineered (phishing) attacks
- Encryption – Cryptographically protect sensitive data and communications
- Policies and procedures - Guidance for employees on what is, and is not, expected of them

- Training - Educate employees on good cybersecurity habits, and how to spot social engineering attacks like phishing scams
- Legal agreements with clients and vendors - Spell out the expectations and limits of liability for each party with regard to sensitive data and cybersecurity
- Intellectual property protection - patent, copyright, trade secret, etc.
- Regulatory compliance - Identify and adhere to relevant regulations

The goal for prevention is not to achieve perfect safety. The goal is to make it hard enough that the vast majority of hackers will turn their attention and effort elsewhere. Larger companies have already done this, which is why hackers are turning to less well protected small- and medium-sized businesses.

Preparedness

As an executive, you can contribute a lot to preparedness without needing a technical background. This is because much of preparedness lies in thinking long-term about problems such as managing cash flow, defending against legal action, purchasing insurance, and saving the company's public image. This kind of broad, forward thinking is precisely what executives are good at, and where they should be contributing to cybersecurity management.

In earlier steps of the cybersecurity plan, your tactical advisors assessed exposure and impact as well as vulnerabilities.

Exposure refers to the types of damages, including collateral damage like lawsuits, that might occur in the wake of an attack. Impact is an assessment of just how bad that damage would be. This forms a backdrop against which you will plan the organization's survival in the wake of an attack. In doing so, you may consider things like:

- Lost productivity - Idle employees who are still getting paychecks
- Lost revenue - Clients defect, and prospective clients turn elsewhere
- Sales pipeline recovery - What will you have to spend to draw prospectives back?
- Lawsuits - Even if you win, the cost of defense can be considerable
- Regulatory fines - Again, the cost of defense, even if you are in the right, is an issue
- Media responses - The cost of managing the organization's public image
- Cleanup - The cost of extra people and experts to contain and clean up the breach
- Workforce - Replacing employees that quit, or must be let go to reduce short-term costs
- Morale - Insecure employees and the cost to convince them they are safe

What will it take to recover from these kinds of post-attack problems? Might a few well-placed investments, put in place before the attack, serve to significantly reduce the damage? These are questions that you should encourage your advisory team to think about as they contemplate preparedness.

Below are some examples of what the tactical team might recommend to prepare the company in the event of an attack, despite taking the preventive measures outlined above. It is not an exhaustive list, and solutions will vary from company to company. The outline is presented to help you understand the types of preparedness controls your team will consider.

Detect

- Intrusion detection system - Systems that detect anomalies in data, traffic, etc. that signal a company may have been compromised. This includes anti-virus scans and spam filtering
- Virus scanning - Detects rogue software on your systems
- Audits and controls - To detect (un)intentional insider wrongdoing
- Audit logs - Keep system logfiles of access, anomalies, etc.

Respond

- Incident response plan - Clear instructions covering how IT responds to the technical issues, when law enforcement gets notified, how management will handle public relations, etc.
- Manage cash flow - Expenses will rise sharply, employees may sit idle, revenue will likely fall, and legal expenses will mount. How will the company pay for these expenses?
- Financial contingencies - Lines of credit, and other sources of operating capital.

- Legal disclosures - Know the company's legal obligations to report certain types of data breaches. These vary by state, and clients in other states can make your company subject to their home state's laws.
- Communication - Coordinate staff, vendors, and external service providers.

Recover
- Data backups - Complete copies of software and data allowing systems to be reset to a known, clean state.
- Regulatory audits - Document compliance with current relevant regulations.
- Legal defense - What will a legal defense cost, and what can a skilled attorney tell you to do in advance of an attack to help limit liability and damages?
- Policies and procedures - Inform everyone of their roles and responsibilities.
- Cyber insurance - A policy, or rider, that covers legal fees, lost productivity, etc. in the event of an attack.
- Public relations - How will customers (new and existing) and the general public perceive the incident, and the company's ability to handle a crisis?
- Sales and marketing - How will scared clients, and prospectives, be won back?
- Improvement - Incorporate lessons learned.

Earlier we described the aftermath of a cyber attack as a perfect storm of cash flowing out while revenue declines and new orders dwindle. The cash flow storm can rage on for months or even years, during which time the organization needs to keep going.

You will be hard pressed to locate sources of cash in the aftermath of an attack. Will it be insurance, lines of credit, or investments of cash from the owner's pocket? The answer will likely be the combination of all three. Some of these sources of revenue may already be in place, and perhaps just need to be expanded where necessary. Determining where cash will come from *before* it is needed is what makes preparation important.

The faster a cybersecurity storm is brought under control, the better chance the business will survive. The end of the storm means the cash flow crisis is over and focus can shift back to profits. Therefore, anything that can shorten the timeline of an attack is worthy of consideration. For example, an attack on a company can go on for months (often over a year) before it is even detected. Good detection controls will help start the process of recovery sooner rather than later, which limits the amount of damage done before cleanup starts. Make sure your advisor's tactical plan considers ways to shorten the timeline of an attack. With regard to timelines, some points to consider include:

- The time a hacker has access to a system before anyone even knows.
- The consulting costs related to clean up and recover.
- The idle time of employees during cleanup and recovery.
- The time customers must wait to place an order, or receive goods and services.
- The speed with which lawsuits and regulatory investigations can be resolved.
- The time before the organization can address the public with facts and action plans.

The vast majority of items on the preparedness list are things that must be in place before the attack occurs, and often help with prevention as well. For instance, employee policies not only reduce risk, but they can reduce liability for an incident as well. To harvest those benefits the policies should be in place before the attack occurs. After the fact, you cannot buy insurance or revise contracts. Prevention and preparedness go hand in hand, and are an important part of your cybersecurity management plan. Consider that as much as one-third of the cost of a cybersecurity attack comes from indirect expenses that pile up after an attack. Indirect costs include employees' time, effort and other organizational resources spent notifying victims and investigating the incident, as well as the loss of goodwill and customer churn.[15]. Since they represent the lion's share of your potential losses, you should spend commensurately to reduce that exposure so that when everyone's best efforts fail, the company will survive.

Regulatory Pressures on Prevention and Preparedness

Checklist-based regulations tend to over-emphasize prevention. There is little room for balancing, because regulatory groups provide an auditable list of things the organization often must have or do to be compliant. As we discussed earlier, the regulations are designed to protect the regulatory group, not necessarily your business. And emphasizing prevention ignores the preparedness part of the equation. By itself, regulatory compliance will almost always leave your security investments unbalanced.

Sometimes regulations allow for alternate controls, which allow an organization to bypass a given requirement for some legitimate reason. The regulation may not be applicable to your

---

[15] "Cost of Data Breach Study: Global Overview," Ponemon Institute, 2017

organization or you may use a different mechanism to control the risk. Generally, the justification for using an alternate control is that it must make sense and accomplish the intent of the regulation. It must also be documented with management signing off on the change. If they are available, alternate controls are a good option when regulations overemphasize prevention. Be sure to direct your tactical advisors to find and use flexibility clauses in regulations to help balance prevention and preparedness in the overall picture.

Shaping a Strategic Plan

At this point, a strategic plan that reflects your company's risk profile is starting to take shape. With it, you are poised to go far beyond asking your IT guru: "Are we safe?" Instead, you have a clearly articulated set of goals and milestones that a diverse team of tactical experts can drive toward. A frosty beverage to celebrate your progress might be in order, as you have already contributed heavily toward managing your organization's risk. If you report to a higher authority, such as a board of directors, you can show them that you are *managing* the organization's cyber risk by presenting the following, and leading them in a discussion about prevention versus preparedness.

- Goals G1 through G5 (Table 2.1)
- Your three-stage process for managing cyber risk illustrated in Figure 2.B
- Milestones M1 through M6 (Table 2.3)
- The output of a strategic cyber risk assessment (Table 3.1)
- A list of the functional areas that must be addressed (Table 4.1)

Once you get approval to move forward (if you need approval beyond yourself) the same information will need to be presented to the tactical advisors you are about to assemble. Collectively the above information will help the tactical team understand your needs and provide them with answers to questions like: "What areas of risk are most important to the company, and how much time/effort should we spend researching solutions for you?"

In short, you are now ready to assemble and engage a diverse tactical team of experts. You also have the knowledge, tools, and strategies to ensure the tactical advisors stays on track. After the team does their part of investigating exposure, impact, and vulnerability, you will use their findings to complete the strategic plan.

Chapter Five

———

Tactical Risk Management

You are now ready to engage a diverse team of tactical expert advisors. This represents a potential transition point where primary responsibility may change from the strategically focused executive to the tactical experts. As you read through this chapter, depending on your role with the company, you will learn either how to manage your tactical team, or what you need to know to be a part of it.

M3: Engage the Tactical Team

It should be clear by now that your tactical cybersecurity team is going to consist of a lot more than just IT staff and technology vendors. In mid-sized companies, the team will include employees who are the advisors to the executive team on things like IT, legal, finance, and other matters. However, in very small companies those advisory roles are typically mentors or vendors. For instance, a small company will tap its insurance agent as team a member to represent that field. A solo-entrepreneur might even tap himself or herself to do some tactical research in areas where external advisors are not available.

You will also find that not every team member needs to be engaged every time the risk plan is executed. However, we highly recommend including the entire advisory team at some point, for example, in cases where the objective is exploring risk. A narrower objective, like Controlling Cost, might require only a few members to work on it. A full team might include someone representing all the functions bulleted below.

- The executive sponsor - You wearing your CEO hat to monitor progress
- Legal advisors - Specialists in intellectual property and legal aspects of cybersecurity
- Insurance advisors - Specialists in cyber insurance
- IT staff and vendors - The front line folks and you, if IT is your thing
- Banking and financial advisors - Advisors for crisis-ready cash flow management
- Public relations and marketing - Specialists who can draft responses for media, clients, and vendors
- Local law enforcement - Who to contact, when it is appropriate, and what to expect
- Cybersecurity specialists - Experts to provide risk management guidance and specialty risk controls
- Sales and marketing - Professionals to help with recovery of revenue stream, and sales pipeline

The first time the advisors are engaged may be intimidating or overwhelming. Team members, especially those outside of IT and cybersecurity, will need to spend time researching the high-level threats to understand how they can reduce those risks. With this in mind, the first engagement might be a roundtable discussion to present the objective and the findings of the strategic cyber risk assessment. This can be followed by a period of research, after which the advisory team meets again. Your meetings might also be less formal, such as a series of discussions over coffee, or through email, with each tactical advisor. While there is some advantage to having everyone in the same room, it is not a requirement.

The first engagement of a broad team may present other challenges as well. For one, the output of the risk assessment may be challenged. This is not necessarily a bad thing. Identifying and reconciling these differences is precisely what aligns strategic objectives with tactical operations. Just don't get hung up on it at this stage. Budgeting and planning, discussed in the next two chapters, are more appropriate places to discuss the differences. Sometimes even at this stage, your advisors will be vying for a slice of the cybersecurity budget. Remember that no matter how confident an advisor may seem or how great a product sounds, nothing will truly prevent all attacks. This is where a strong leader with a good understanding of the strategic plan will help keep things under control.

Another challenge of the first meeting is that the advisory team will produce a lot of ideas, suggestions, and information that must be digested. Do your best to keep the discussion focused. Once the dust settles, advisory meetings will give way to a series of routine check-ins that just cover changes and new findings in their respective areas of expertise When this happens, it means the organization has adopted cybersecurity as part of its culture.

M4: Tactical Assessments

While the strategic cyber risk assessment provides a look at your organization's strategic footprint, a tactical assessment fills in the specifics. To create a solid cybersecurity plan you need to use both a strategic and tactical risk assessment in your planning process.

Inventory - The Tactical Footprint

The process of working through milestone M4, Tactical Assessments, starts with an inventory of sensitive data and the systems that contain, transmit, or process it. The goal is to catalog the kinds of data the organization captures, processes, and keeps. The first time you or your team works through this will be somewhat time-consuming, but things will go a lot faster during subsequent times. Future inventories are just a matter of adding, removing, and updating the catalog that was created initially.

Your catalog's size will depend on your business. A lone consultant working from home may have a relatively short list, but most organizations will have a fairly long list. Regardless of the size of the business, one thing that can be said with a high level of confidence is that the list will be much longer than you expect. Those claiming they are "not an Internet company" will be shocked to learn just how connected and exposed they really are.

The order in which the inventory is performed makes little difference, but starting with data is a good choice. Regardless of the order chosen, it is likely that working through one will trigger thoughts about the others. You may even try to work through them simultaneously. Do what feels natural and what fits the team best.

Following is a list of things that should be included in your inventory:

Data
- Employee data
- Customer data
- Financial/banking data
- Vendor/contractor data
- Sensitive knowledge and know how
- Internal, external, and privileged communication
- Image and culture
- Specific skills and education

Systems
- Financial and accounting
- Ad hoc systems - Spreadsheets, file sharing
- Enterprise, management and specialty systems - ERP, CRM, CAD, etc.

Devices
- Physical storage of physical information - File cabinets, home offices, vehicles
- Personal computing - Cash registers, smartphones, laptops, tablets, etc.
- Data storage, processing and recovery - Backups, portable storage, and cloud systems
- Communication devices - Phones, LAN's, WiFi, etc.

Services
- Banking and financial
- Internet providers
- Website hosting servers
- Cloud/software as a service

You can visit the website[16] for this book to get worksheets that help with the inventory process. The worksheets outline the most commonly captured data, the most common systems, typical devices, and services that small companies might employ. You can use them as a guide to get started, and extend them with items that are unique to your organization.

Emerging Systems and Technologies

One of the most frustrating aspects of cybersecurity is that the landscape is constantly changing. One force that drives change is the emergence of new systems and new technologies. When new gadgets and services first enter the scene, they often creep slowly into our lives, and our business, without anyone paying much attention. Because they are not very mature, they often lack good (or any) security controls. The lack of security controls makes them attractive from a productivity standpoint, but they often leave data very exposed. Inevitably, hackers and criminals recognize the opportunity to exploit these new pathways.

For example, the first wave of smartphones and tablets were very insecure. As emerging technologies, they weren't built with the same security controls that experts had developed for mainframes

---

[16] Download companion material from http://CybersecurityABusinessSolution.com

and desktop computers. But as time went on they were forced to adopt basic security controls. Cloud computing, Software As A Service, and other technologies have followed this path too. In all cases, they left in their wake several costly security breaches for the unlucky few that adopted the trend early and paid the price for not managing the risk of being on the leading edge.

At the time this book is being written, the Internet of Things (IoT), aerial drones, and wearable computing are among the emerging technologies that are extremely vulnerable. In addition, smart TVs, smart thermostats, and other devices are constantly gathering data, which may result in an unexpected breach of confidentiality. Always on, always listening devices designed to be in-home, digital assistants currently lack many basic controls, like password protection. These devices currently make your calendar, contacts, and other information available to anyone who asks. Augmented reality devices that capture and expose private information are another emerging issue. Sometimes the risks are apparent, but sometimes they remain hidden (and exploited) for years.

The best way to deal with emerging devices, systems, and technologies is to periodically review your organization's inventory of data, systems, and devices. The recommended frequency for this kind of checkup is once a year. Knowing what devices are in use helps you make informed decisions about the trade-off between novel devices and the risks they may present.

After a brief inventory of data, systems, and devices, the team's next goal is to assess how those elements expose the company. Exposure includes legal and regulatory considerations, which are largely driven by external forces.

Regulatory and Legal Exposure

Industry and data-specific regulations combine with a patchwork of federal, state, and international laws to create a tangled web of requirements and responsibilities for many businesses and organizations. Similar to emerging technologies, they are constantly shifting and changing. In fact, the emergence of new technologies is the biggest driver of changes in the regulatory and legal landscape.

One reason the tactical team includes members from legal, financial, and insurance backgrounds is to make sure the necessary knowledge is presented to advise you on this perspective of exposure. If the organization is innocently unaware, it will be too late to make the company compliant after an attack. Ignorance is not an excuse, and it is definitely not bliss, when the company faces fines and lawsuits.

Share the inventories of data, systems, and devices with trusted advisors in their respective fields. Ask them to identify relevant regulations and to explain the current legal landscape. In particular, the legal advice gathered here is used in the planning and implementation stages to significantly reduce organizational risk.

A few common regulations and regulatory bodies that impact small businesses include:

- Payment Card Industry Data Security Standard (PCI DSS)
- Health Insurance Portability and Accountability Act (HIPAA or HIPAA-HITECH)

- Federal Information Security Management Act of 2002 (FISMA)
- The North American Electric Reliability Corporation (NERC)
- Federal Financial Institutions Examination Council (FFIEC)
- DFARS 225.204-7012 / NIST SP 800-171
- The Gramm-Leach-Bliley Act (GLBA)

It is also important to note that, in addition to federal laws, each state has particular requirements regarding data privacy and data breach disclosure requirements. Data breach disclosure means you must report any attack on your company that compromises certain sensitive data. Failure to do so can expose the organization to fines and class action lawsuits. You may even be held personally liable for negligence. Complicating the matter further, the state laws that apply are often based on your client's location, not just your company's location, so make sure you are aware of all laws that might apply.

Regulatory Self-Audit

Another part of milestone M4 is performing any regulatory self-audits, but you can skip it if your organization is lucky enough not to be subject to any regulations. Sometimes there is a special checklist for a self-audit. Other times the audit itself is just done "in pencil." Either way, the objective at this point is to figure out what needs to be done to pass a full audit. Later, as part of the implementation milestone, the audit will be done "in ink," or by a third party, to achieve and document compliance.

Contract and Policy Review

In the course of doing business, you will enter into a number of contractual obligations. It is important to review these agreements from time to time to make sure you understand the obligations into which you have entered. Anywhere liability can be transferred, or limited, should be noted for the future. Severe contractual problems may warrant making an immediate change. Smaller issues may be handled at contract renewal time, and may become part of your vendor selection process. Your attorney, financial advisor, and insurance agent can help you with areas of concern outlined below, and advise you in areas specific to your organization.

Employees
- Confidentiality
- Privacy
- Policies and procedures

Client and vendors
- Confidentiality
- Safeguarding data
- Data ownership
- Privacy and data sharing
- Service level agreements for degraded/delayed service
- Data theft/exposure liability and indemnification

Banking
- Liability for external fraud
- Liability for internal fraud (employee, or insider, theft)

Insurance
- Requirements to maintain coverage
- Claim limits

Assessing Tactical Impact

This is one area where tactical advisers can get bogged down in the details. Trying to assign a specific dollar value to every type of data, every system, and every device can be incredibly time-consuming. In some cases, the information needed to calculate a precise dollar figure would require revealing sensitive information to members of the team who may not need to know such things. Furthermore, business value is spread across data, systems, devices, and services that are tightly integrated with one another such that specific values are almost impossible to pin down. For these reasons, it is better for small companies to use a more abstract approach and course measurements to keep the process moving along quickly. The three main ways data is compromised are defined as:

- Confidentiality - Private (client, employee, trade secret) information in the wrong hands
- Integrity - Loss, destruction, or tampering with information
- Accessibility - An inability to access, process, or communicate information

For each type of compromise, consider the following impact perspectives:

- Lost sales
- Productivity decline
- Legal and contractual requirements
- Tarnished public image
- Cleanup and recovery expenses
- Defending lawsuits
- Regulatory penalties

When trying to estimate the cost of each impact, consider these value viewpoints:

- Value to your organization (market value, replacement value, operational value)
- Value to society (disruption of power, water, food, healthcare)
- Value to the client, patient, or employee to whom it belongs
- Value to an adversary (blackmail, insider trading, competitor intelligence)

For example, consider employee W-2 data in terms of confidentiality. It has some, but probably minimal, operational value to the organization. Adversarial hackers find enough value to make it worth trying to steal, but the main source of value comes from the employee to whom the data belongs. If sensitive employee data is lost, it probably will not do much to affect sales, but it could trigger losses in any of the other impact categories. An attorney or human resources specialist will have a good perspective on how high the damage might go for your situation, which illustrates the need for a diverse team of experts. In a medium-sized company, this process might take the form of a round-table discussion. A solo entrepreneur is more likely to email someone they know, or search the Internet for answers.

Assessing Tactical Vulnerability

Vulnerability assessments are a collection of tactical tools designed to identify flaws and backdoors that a hacker might exploit. They examine containers and conduits of information for flaws without consideration to the value of the information inside them. A backdoor into a non-critical system is not the same as a backdoor into a confidential medical records system. This is how vulnerability relates to impact. One measures the container, the other measure what is inside the container. Examples of vulnerability assessments include:

- Penetration Tests - An attempt to break into systems by jiggling the locks to see which doors will open. Common aliases: Pen-tests, Red Team Assessments
- Patch Scan - An inventory of software and firmware version numbers used to determine which systems are missing critical software updates. Common aliases: Patch Inventory, Hardware/Software or System Inventory
- Vulnerability Scan - A combination of all of the above. A database of known exploits for each system drives a systematic probe for flaws, known vulnerabilities, rogue software, viruses, missing software patches, and configuration issues. Common aliases: Network Scan, Configuration Audit, Website Scan, Virus Scan

Most vulnerability assessments will only attempt to identify known flaws, backdoors, and misconfigurations. Sophisticated versions can sometimes find previously unknown flaws. Most small businesses just need the basic versions, primarily as a matter of cost. The exception might be a major system, which holds all the company's eggs in one basket. In that case, a high-end vulnerability assessment might be worth the expense.

Vulnerability assessments tend to produce long lists of flaws, which are coded according to severity. They differ from strategic cyber risk assessments in that severity is contextual to the container and not the business impact. How the tool defines severity is something to consider when selecting among the available options, and helps with interpreting the results.

Sharing the Results

Once your tactical advisory team has worked through milestone M4, they should prepare a summary of the information to share with management. Of course, if you are the only executive and you participated in the above steps, you need not report them to yourself. However, you will want to step back and consider how these discoveries might reshape your strategic point of view.

Summarizing the data, systems, and devices will show where intangible values reside. Reporting exposure involves explaining how bad things could get if an attack materializes, and a summary of vulnerability will show where the weak spots are in terms of preventing attacks on high impact areas.

Whether you create a formal report, or just have a moment of reflection as a sole owner/operator, the goal is to compare the tactical footprint with the strategic footprint. Do they align with one another? Does the tactical view change or influence the executive's perspective of the strategic landscape?

In conclusion, assemble a broad tactical team to look closely at all your risks. Confidentiality, accessibility, and integrity are the lenses through which the team should be examining granular risks. Your job is to guide the team, not wade into the details. Use the output of the strategic cyber risk assessment to direct the team's effort into the areas of greatest importance. Ask the team to examine the details of each threat category from their own professional perspective and report back where the weaknesses and impact are greatest.

Chapter Six

———

Budget Planning

The exposure, impact, and vulnerability exercises discussed in Chapter Five will help your tactical team uncover what is at stake. These exercises also provide you with information about the estimated costs associated with cybersecurity and cyber attacks. Expect the numbers to be jaw-dropping, perhaps to the point of disbelief, but they are undoubtedly quite real. Exposure to the after-effects of a cyber attack is staggering. Maintaining payroll, fending off lawsuits, and winning back clients whose trust has been shaken while revenue falls can easily bankrupt an unprepared business.

The exercises from the previous chapter culminate in summaries of tactical findings that can be added to the simple plan we started with in Table 3.1. Table 6.1 shows how the tactical team's impact assessments might be assembled alongside the strategic plan. In this example, we assume the tactical team uncovered a regulatory requirement and advised addressing it first because there were steep legal exposures that could bankrupt the organization. The addition of an objective and re-prioritizing the strategic plan based on tactical information is to be expected. It is part of the process illustrated in Figure 2.A that helps unravel the dilemma of needing both strategic and tactical information to make good decisions.

Table 6.1 – Example of a strategic cyber risk management plan taking shape.

Objective	Priority	Budget Allocation	Potential Damage
Regulatory Compliance – Meet PCI DSS Requirements	1	?	$430k
Reduce Risk – Website Attacks	2	66%	$240k
Reduce Risk – Point of Sale Hacks	3	34%	$320k

The plan has clear objectives and clear priorities. However, some data is missing and you may wonder why the budget allocation and potential damages do not line up. The reason is that the budget allocations reflect a strategic view of the risk landscape and potential damage represents the tactical view. That they would differ is not cause for alarm, but rather cause for discussion. Perhaps there is a legitimate reason for the deviation, such as the existence of antiquated systems that require more protection than newer ones. If this is the case, perhaps you would consider an upgrade rather than more security measures. This is another example of the interaction between strategic and tactical decision making and underscores your role in facilitating communication.

The tactical team could split into smaller groups to begin tackling each objective, but there are still unanswered questions. How much of the budget should get shifted into the regulatory objective? And how much should the overall budget be? This chapter guides you toward setting a cybersecurity budget that makes sense.

Budget Allocation

The strategic cyber risk assessment offers suggestions for allocating budgets among multiple threats to make sure all the bases are covered. It also helps organizations align spending on cybersecurity with the strategic objectives set by top management. Allocations according to the risk assessment will also help you make investments in reducing risk that reflect the external cyber threat landscape.

While it does represent the lion's share of the budget, reducing risk related to major threat categories are not the only the only objectives that need funding. Stage one of the risk management process in Figure 2.B, exploring the risk to develop a plan and figure out what should be spent, must also be funded. Any mandatory regulations must also be met and those costs are relatively fixed. Examining risk to reduce costs also comes with a price tag, as do opportunities for gaining profit or market share. Finally, as discussed at length in Chapter Four, you will need to allocate spending between prevention and preparedness.

Table 6.2 is a guide to how the cybersecurity budget is allocated at its highest levels. The last column indicates when in the cyber risk management cycle you should be prepared to realize the expense.

Table 6.2 – Long-term risk management guide.

Objective	Allocation	Strategy	When
Exploring Risk	5-10%	Measure exposure and set risk appetite	Annually, or when major changes occur
Regulatory Compliance	Fixed Cost	Meet requirements, leverage alternate controls	Driven by audit cycle
Reducing Risk	Risk Based	The risk assessment, risk appetite, and residual risk management. Split between prevention and preparedness.	As dictated by exploring risk
Controlling Costs	< 5%	Reduce costs by a target amount, without too much risk	Bad Times
Identifying Opportunities	Unlimited	Increase profits or gain market share	Good Times

The cost of regulatory compliance will be driven by the audit requirements attached to them. Taking steps to reduce risk will be driven by multiple strategies, which are discussed shortly. If revenue falls during bad times, then taking action to control costs makes sense. When times are good, you can look for opportunities in the risk landscape that push the organization ahead of the competition. These last two scenarios will be discussed in the next chapter, but they deserve mention in the context of allocating resources.

Budget Sizing

In addition to allocation, the overall size of the budget needs to be set. Current research establishes 37 percent of the expected loss as the point of diminishing return.[17] Expected loss is the likelihood that an attack will occur multiplied by the amount of damage suffered in the attack. You will recall the risk formulas in Chapter Two calculated these figures. In the example, a given company had a 20 percent chance of Threat X incurring $1M dollars of damage, so its expected loss is $200k. According to the research, $74k ($200k X 37%) would be the academic ceiling on expenditure.

Of course, 37 percent is a theoretical limit, and there are multiple risks to address, which means applying that formula is not exactly straightforward. The practical limit is more like the break-even point when pricing goods and services. The cost to produce a product or service cannot cost more than its selling price. Likewise, the costs of cybersecurity cannot exceed the losses it protects. In an ideal world, we would calculate the break-even point for every

---

[17] Gordon, L., Loeb, M., Lucyshyn, W. and Zhou, L., "Externalities and the Magnitude of Cyber Security Underinvestment by Private Sector Firms: A Modification of the Gordon-Loeb Model." *Journal of Information Security*, 6, 24-30. doi: 10.4236/jis.2015.61003. 2015.

possible cybersecurity investment and then find solutions that cost that much or less. However, this type of cost-benefit analysis for every scenario is simply too much to ask of a small company.

A simpler way to approach sizing the overall cybersecurity budget is to think of it like buying car insurance. You first determine the amount of risk, which is what we worked through in the previous chapters. Then you buy as much coverage as you can afford without giving up too much of the profits.

The final amount your organization decides to spend on cybersecurity will be unique to your organization. It will depend on cultural aspects of the organization, such as the management team's aversion to risk. For example, a company that wants to be a leader in protecting client data will budget far more than a company that is seeking market share as a low-cost leader. This leads to the topic of *risk appetite*. Again, using our car insurance metaphor, risk appetite is like picking a deductible amount. A higher deductible means you pay a lower premium, but you have to pay more out of pocket when a claim is filed. While not a perfect correlation to risk appetite, it an easy way to grasp the concept.

Ultimately, you need to back into a budget size by figuring out how much it will cost to bring your organization's exposure in line with the company's risk appetite. This is another example of a chicken-or-egg dilemma that must be untangled. It will require some amount of back and forth between the strategic and tactical strategies depicted in Figure 2.A. In other words, you will propose a rough budget using the strategic data, then have the tactical advisory team present solution options that reduce as much risk as possible given the budget constraints. There may be places where changing the rough budget you set makes sense based on the cost and effectiveness of the team's proposed solutions.

To establish a rough budget, work your way through the objectives based on their strategic priority. For each, the potential damages are the total amount of risk that needs to be managed. Subtract from this amount the organization's appetite for risk. That might include free cash, credit lines, standby investments (i.e. an owner's infusion of cash in a crisis), and any cyber insurance coverage that would offset those losses. The cost of maintaining these risk appetite components is your first budget item. The potential losses, less the risk appetite, is the *residual risk*.

Building on the example in Table 6.1, take $430k as the starting value. Subtract $100k from that, which is represents cash and an emergency line of credit that could be tapped in the event of a crisis. Also, subtract $30k which is the limit of the organization's current insurance coverage in the event of a cybersecurity incident[18]. Residual risk is now $300k. The cash and line of credit cost nothing to maintain. The insurance agent advises that the existing cybersecurity coverage adds only $300 per year to the premium. The insurance premium for coverage is added as the first line item in the rough budget.

In the case of mandatory regulations[19], you will need to allocate enough of your budget to reach compliance, and then stay

---

[18] General business liability policies often (but not always) include some small amount of coverage for data breach, or cybersecurity, events. If such coverage exists it is unlikely to be enough, but use what you have.

[19] Voluntary risks are considered later, as an opportunity cost.

compliant. Your tactical advisory team will research the costs associated with meeting mandatory requirements. The advisors should also present guidance on how meeting the regulations will reduce overall risk. For instance, being compliant might allow for the reduction or elimination of fines. Compliance may also bring down the risk of losses in a lawsuit. Whatever these reductions are, add them up and subtract them from the residual risk.

In our example, the tactical team reported that complying with PCI DSS regulations would reduce the current risk by $150k because fines and major lawsuits could be avoided. They estimated the cost to comply at $10k upfront and $2k annually. Residual risk is now $150k and the budget gets new line items of $10k for this year and $2k going forward for PCI compliance.

Here the value of cybersecurity investments begins to take shape. In exchange for an upfront fee of $10k and $2k annually thereafter, the organization can reduce their risk by an additional $150k. If there were a second proposal that cost more but reduced the risk even further, then it might be the better choice. Perhaps the higher cost is because the second solution bundled additional recovery services that the less expensive solution did not include. By investigating the reduction in overall risk for each solution, you will have the information you need to make good investment decisions. Justifying cybersecurity investments, even if you are only justifying them to yourself, is important. No one likes spending money without understanding what they get in return.

The same process follows for each remaining threat. Begin with the total potential damages, subtract the organization's appetite for risk and any existing insurance that might apply.

Sometimes the same line item applies across multiple risks. For instance, the general liability policy that offers $30k of cybersecurity insurance might apply to every type of attack. Thus, the $300 annual premium for that line item only gets counted once in the budget, even though the reduction of risk applies to multiple risk scenarios. This will be an iterative process which continues until the strategic and tactical advisors are all happy with the outcome. The result is a list of residual risks that looks something like Table 6.3.

Table 6.3 – Example of a strategic cyber risk management plan taking shape.

Objective	Residual Risk
Regulatory Compliance – Meet PCI DSS Requirements	$150k
Reduce Risk – Website Attacks	$160k
Reduce Risk – Point of Sale Hacks	$100k

You will then turn to your legal, financial, and insurance advisors for discussions about how best to deal with these residual risks. The strategic cyber risk assessment will also be helpful in giving context to these pockets of risk.

- Can they be contractually transferred, avoided, or limited?
- Does a larger source of emergency cash/credit make sense?
- Should insurance coverage be revised?

If you report to a higher authority, such as a board of
directors, these are the kinds of decisions that should be presented
to them for discussion. If the buck stops with you, then just choose
the path that lets you sleep best at night. The correct way to deal
with residual risk will, as we mentioned above, depend on the
company's culture, aversion to risk, and other factors that are
unique to every organization.

Funding the budget is another hurdle. Table 6.4 presents the
typical budget sources for each objective.

Table 6.4 – Funding sources.

Objective	Funding Source
Exploring Risk	Overhead
Regulatory Compliance	Overhead or cost of goods/services sold
Reducing Risk	Overhead or cost of goods/services sold
Controlling Costs	Savings from reduced cost
Identifying Opportunities	Increased profit and/or volume

Exploring risk is an overhead cost and, because it examines
the entire company, should be spread across all products and
services. Regulatory and risk reduction objectives can either be
company-wide initiatives (overhead), or they can be a specific cost
of producing a particular product/service. Controlling costs
requires at least an up-front investment of time, but that
investment will be recovered in the savings that result. Likewise,
the up-front investments required to take advantage of

opportunities is recovered from the higher profits or higher volumes that result. We will talk more about cost controls and opportunities in the next chapter.

In summary, the executive's role in planning is to keep the tactical advisory team focused and build a budget. The plan and budget should adhere to strategic priorities and incorporate tactical findings. Regulatory constraints are generally fixed, but some compliance solutions will do a better job of lowering risk than others. The overall size of the budget will be defined by risk appetite, solutions that reduce risk, and the cost of dealing with residual risk. Any regulatory constraints represent fixed costs within the budget and opportunities will push the cybersecurity budget higher.

Chapter Seven

———

Implementation and Beyond

M6: Implementation

Now that you've worked through setting an objective, exploring risk, and allocating a budget, it's time for implementation. This final milestone sets the plan into motion. Whether you are the one implementing solutions or it is being handled by the tactical team, there will be some things that require executive involvement, such as:

- Communication both inside and outside of the organization
- Audits that require signatures from the top executives
- Support for policies drafted by the tactical team
- Contract revisions that require executive negotiation with clients or vendors
- Constant improvements to the plan and implementing lessons learned

Communication. The overarching role of the executive is communication. The process of guiding, listening, and making adjustments should continue through the implementation stage. Despite the best-laid plans, the advisory team may uncover new challenges during implementation. The executive's door should remain open throughout implementation to address any unknowns that arise.

A diverse team of advisors, each speaking their own jargon, may require executive intervention to facilitate communication between team members. In addition to language barriers, turf battles and other conflicts can derail an implementation. This fact underscores the need to keep objectives very narrow.

You may also need to coordinate communication with other employees. Putting tactical solutions in place can disrupt normal routines to which other employees and vendors have become accustomed. Supporting the team's efforts, especially when they are not well received, is clearly an executive role. The same applies when changes are disruptive or ill received by clients. Someone has to wade into these situations to explain the reasoning and smooth any ruffled feathers. That someone is likely to be you.

Audits. Most audits require executive-level signatures, but be careful not to blindly sign documents. Make sure the responsible employees and vendors actually did what the audit claims. Paying lip-service to audits may be a short-term win, but trying to defend that position in a lawsuit after the fact can be costly.

Supporting Policies. Policies are just pieces of paper until the weight of the executive team is behind them. The executive sets the tone and establishes the culture that defines an organization's attitude toward policies and procedures. Your attorney, staff, and vendors may write cybersecurity policies, but creating a culture that embraces them is something only you can do for the organization. Only the top-most executives have the power and authority to promote a culture that values protecting the organization. Of course, culture is a two-way street. Sometimes well-meaning policies, procedures, or regulatory requirements can become a burden to the people who are tasked with adopting them. Recognizing legitimate issues and facilitating good communication is how efficiencies and opportunities within the risk landscape are found.

Client/Supplier Contract Revisions. Even the most diligent cybersecurity efforts can crumble when things go wrong in a related organization. The supply chain, and the company's position in a larger supply chain, shape organizational strategy. Supplier relationships and liability to clients play a significant role in defining high-level cyber risk. The written and unwritten aspects of these relationships are worthy of your attention.

Consider the 2013 credit card heist at Target, which resulted in 40 million credit card numbers being stolen. The start of the attack was traced back to network credentials used by a refrigeration, heating and air conditioning subcontractor. All of Target's main cybersecurity controls got bypassed because a member of their supply chain fell prey to a phishing attack, which gave the attackers a way in. The result was a nightmare for Target. When the story of the subcontractor's involvement broke in the *Wall Street Journal*, that nightmare extended to the subcontractor as well.

It is worth your time to consider supply chain relationships, and the liability that flows through them. Contracts should spell out each party's responsibility. In doing so, opportunities for gain may emerge. Accepting more risk may command higher profit margins, and having an excellent cyber risk management plan becomes a selling point. Executives that manage supply chain risk well can surpass their competition.

Constant Improvements. The executive has another key role to consider, which is coordinating the recovery and response phases of a cyber crisis. Well prepared executives will have a plan in place for communicating with key assets in a crisis. They will be ready to manage external communication with law enforcement, press, and regulatory entities.

A good way to get prepared and figure out what might be needed in a crisis is with drills. These can be elaborate enactments of an event, or they can be paper-based tabletop exercises. The simplest form, which may be all a solo-entrepreneur needs, is a mental drill. Simply thinking through major threat scenarios and considering what you would do, who you would contact, and what you might say to the press is an invaluable exercise.

Another way is to learn from your organization's own mistakes (hopefully small ones) that will inevitably get made along the way. Stuff happens, but we can learn from that stuff. We can also learn from others and from experts in the field. This includes talking with peers and noting emerging cybersecurity trends within the industry.

Managing Cybersecurity Over Time

Over time, your company's strategic and financial circumstances will change. Company growth, new partnerships, and evolving industry regulations are just a few examples of how the organization changes. Changes are usually slow and subtle, but there can also be dramatic changes, like gaining (or losing) a huge client. New regulations can also change the playing field overnight.

The threat landscape of cybersecurity is forever changing as well. New adversaries emerge that did not previously exist. For instance, hacktivists, or activists that use cyber attacks to shame or damage a company over social issues, were virtually unheard of until recently. The technology we rely on is also ever changing. Smartphones in the workplace have dramatically altered the threat landscape since their introduction. Even if a company makes no changes internally, the world around it will change nonetheless. If there is one thing to be said with certainty, it is that things will change.

The strategic cyber risk assessment is an easy way to detect changes that require action. Performing a risk assessment on a quarterly or annual is recommended, because it will alert you to any change in the external risk landscape. If the output does not change, then the organization can maintain its current course. If the output differs significantly, then the tactical assessments should be repeated in threat categories that have changed.

Strategic changes in the company also indicate when it is time to do a new strategic cyber risk assessment. It may even be helpful to perform the risk assessment ahead of deliberate strategic changes. Doing a risk assessment with *proposed* changes to strategic inputs provides a snapshot of how drastically the risks will change. The difference between the status quo results and the proposed results is helpful for plotting a successful transformation.

Regulatory requirements may also be a trigger for re-evaluating risk. When new regulations or major changes take place, the organization will need to adapt. If the organization is already addressing the major threats as described in this book, then addressing a regulatory change can be a project unto itself. Use the same six milestones, and process as before, but set the objective to Regulatory Compliance to keep the tactical advisory team tightly focused.

It may seem daunting to think you must repeat this process at least annually, but year two is much easier than year one. In subsequent years most of the tactical research and advice is still valid. Instead of re-doing all the work every time, you and the tactical advisors are just addressing major changes.

Chapter Three introduced two potential objectives: Controlling Cost and Identifying Risk. We consider them next as part of the long-term strategy for managing risk. Until an organization has addressed the risk landscape and any mandatory regulations, it should not attempt to achieve any other objectives. As tempting as it may be to roll everything all into one big project, that strategy is highly discouraged. These final two objectives have targets that are 180 degrees from those involved in reducing risk, increasing resilience, or meeting regulations. Deal with the threats and regulations first, then tackle these advanced objectives.

Controlling Cost

Normally, when reducing the risk associated with various threats, the objective is to make some investment of time and money in exchange for a reduction of potential loss. However, scenarios exist in which the approach needs to be reversed. Lean times often means making cuts to operating costs across the board. Sometimes even cybersecurity budgets must be slashed to save jobs or keep a company out of bankruptcy. When that happens, the objective is to find ways to reduce investments in cybersecurity expense in exchange for an increase in risk.

The process follows the same pattern using the same strategies and tools. You begin with a clearly articulated objective to cut costs by some target amount. Then do a strategic cyber risk assessment and ask your tactical advisors to assess what you are *currently* doing to reduce risk. Their evaluation will focus on what happens to exposure, impact, and vulnerability if the organization abandons existing products, services, or efforts. This process allows executives to make informed, rational decisions about where to make cost cuts that do not expose the company to more risk than necessary.

Lean times are not the only trigger for cost control. Consider a company that wants to compete on price by keeping all costs at the bare minimum. An organization with that strategic mission might routinely evaluate cybersecurity spending with the aim of reducing costs without raising risks at all. In this scenario, the tactical advisory team looks for newer, less expensive solutions, or more effective solutions, to see if risk levels could be maintained while squeezing out unnecessary cost.

Cybersecurity: A Business Solution

A company that wishes to distance itself from the competition based on price may find strategic value in controlling cybersecurity costs as part of a larger strategy. However, gaining market share by controlling expenses is only one way to find gains within the cybersecurity landscape.

Identifying Opportunities

Large competitors that have addressed cybersecurity are simply waiting for smaller competitors to fall prey to a cyber attack. The savvy ones have marketing plans ready to entice your customers to switch as soon as they learn about a breach. Some won't even wait for a breach and will simply win clients by sowing seeds of doubt in your ability to protect sensitive data. Security and privacy are important to individual, corporate, and government consumers. Large companies already know this, and they are acting.

Knowing what your clients expect in terms of security is important. For this reason, when the objective is to identify opportunities, your tactical advisory team might include sales, marketing, and customer service advisors. A diverse team can answer questions like:

- Do your clients care about the data you collect?
- How do prospective clients determine if your operations are secure?
- Do clients have current or pending regulatory requirements that vendors must meet?

When clients value the data being collected you can leverage that by investing in above average security controls. Not only will this reduce your risk, but it builds trust and confidence with your clients, which may allow you to charge a premium.

As an example, it costs very little to add "bank grade" encryption to a website, that encrypts everything between your site and your customer's computer or smartphone. Securing every web page may not reduce risk any more than securing just the pages that collect sensitive information, but seeing the little lock icon on the web browser everywhere on your site will give them confidence. It may seem trivial, but banks have used subliminal hints in the form of elaborate vaults and heavy granite architecture to signal strength and security for centuries.

There are more overt ways to establish trust with clients too. A company might adopt a voluntary regulation or certification to win business from clients that require, or see added value in, suppliers that meet a given regulation. In this case, compliance is a badge of trust that opens doors to select clients. Even when it is not a requirement, meeting voluntary regulations increases confidence in the security of a company's internal operations.

There are also some markets that are closed, or will soon be closed, to companies that cannot meet certain cybersecurity regulatory criteria. Banks, medical facilities, and public utilities are a few examples of what the U.S. government refers to as *critical infrastructure.* These are sectors of our economy that have a very low tolerance, or are at very high risk, for cyber attacks. They and their government counterparts, including the department of defense, are starting to require their suppliers to meet certain cybersecurity standards. If your company serves clients in these sectors or serves government entities, getting compliant early gives your company an edge.

Although most of the implementation falls to tactical experts, there are several specific items that require executive action. Managing communication and conflicts between members of the implementation team or between the team and other employees is an important executive duty. Minimizing the potential for conflict is another reason to keep objectives very narrow, and to only address them one at a time. Broad projects put too many cooks in the kitchen.

Following implementation, the executive is responsible for long-term risk management by keeping tabs on the risk landscape. A strategic cyber risk assessment is the easiest way to detect change that requires action. Perform them annually or when there are major changes within the organization. Once regulations and risks have been addressed, and between annual checkups thereof, it may be prudent to investigate opportunities for gain or ways to control cost.

Conclusion

Since the advent of computers, the business world has taken a reactive approach to cybersecurity. When attacks were few and far between this made sense, but the world has changed. The value of data has grown exponentially over the past decades and appears to be accelerating. Unfortunately, growth in value also means growth in liability. That is why cybersecurity boils down to a business problem.

Implementation and Beyond

Businesses have been keen to capitalize on the rapidly increasing value of data. Small and medium businesses are no exception, and have enjoyed this trend right alongside their larger peers. Even the tiniest companies are awash with valuable data because technology has made its collection ubiquitous. A single smartphone contains more data than a room full of computers could handle just a few decades ago. The volume and value of information we can effortlessly collect is truly incredible.

Anytime an economic bubble forms, the downside risk increases in equal measure. The value of information is clearly following this pattern, and the recent surge in cybercrime is just the beginning of the downside. History is about to repeat itself. You can rely on luck or you can manage your way through what we know is coming.

Please visit the website for this book to learn more about the Wild West frontier of cybersecurity. The site contains a wealth of information and tools that were designed to help you understand and navigate the risks small and medium companies face. You will also find downloadable worksheets and companion resources that will help you organize the exploration of your organization's cyber risk.

http://CybersecurityABusinessSolution.com

About the Author

———

     Rob Arnold's passion for computers and technology began when he was a teenager, on computers that predated the modern IBM PC. If you were around in the late 1970s and early 1980s, you may recall names like Commodore, Timex-Sinclair, and Tandy. Rob experienced them all and, like every modern-day teenage boy, he wanted to play video games. While he could not afford the luxury of a lot of games, he did not let that be an obstacle. Instead, he taught himself how to write his own games. These early forays into the world of computing lit a passion that would later define his career. But even before turning his passion into a profession, Rob had his first experience with modern computer security issues. While in college, he was helping his professor manage a small fleet of computers when he discovered a flaw that made brute-force password attacks way too easy for remote hackers. Changing the default installation for the software involved solved the issue and that became Rob's first meaningful contribution to the software systems that underpin our modern Internet.

     Upon entering the professional world of information technology, what is today known as cybersecurity, was then just part of the job. Rob spent two decades working and providing IT consulting, for companies ranging from Fortune 500 and large private firms, to small mom-and-pop shops, and everything in between. During this time, Rob wrote security policies, led companies through security-related compliance audits, and had several opportunities to do what is now called ethical hacking. One defining moment was on the morning of 9-11, when Rob was called to examine and repair the hacking of a major airline-related website that occurred while planes crashed along the East Coast. On other occasions, he was hired to crack systems for which the administrator (or root) password had been lost. Rob has solved many other problems for clients, ranging from securing executive communication from the prying eyes of untrusted IT staffers, to disaster recovery planning, to developing authentication and permission management software.

Rob returned to graduate school in 2010 to round out his real-world experience with an academic view of the cybersecurity landscape. As part of an early assignment, he discovered, and quietly disclosed to the manufacture, a major flaw in a popular e-reader. But what really caught his attention was the concept of risk management as applied to cybersecurity. It was clear to him that risk management and the primary tool for measuring risk (a risk assessment) was well-suited to make investment decisions related to security. For his capstone project, he developed a unique strategic risk assessment that would lay the foundation for his next professional endeavor.

Rob founded Threat Sketch in 2015 and partnered with a financial and insurance risk expert to continue research and development. Their focus is on the development of cyber risk assessments to solve budgeting and planning problems for small and medium businesses. The addition of his business partner's professional risk-analysis knowledge marked the point where academic research transitioned to a practical tool.

Cybersecurity: A Business Solution

The cybersecurity industry is awash with highly-technical advice, guides, and solutions. But there are few resources for business-minded owners and executives who need to understand the business aspects of managing cyber risk. This book distills Rob's practical and academic knowledge to help the leaders and decision-makers of small companies navigate the management of cyber risk. He is particularly in tune with what resources are available to small businesses and how they need to approach cybersecurity. His background helps him understand the unique constraints businesses of this size face, having worked many years in this industry.

———